# SEATTLE MARINERS

## STARS, STATS, HISTORY, AND MORE!

BY CONOR BUCKLEY

**The Child's World®**
childsworld.com

Published by The Child's World®
1980 Lookout Drive • Mankato, MN 56003-1705
800-599-READ • www.childsworld.com

ISBN 9781503828384
LCCN 2018944853

Printed in the United States of America
PAO2392

Photo Credits:
Cover: Joe Robbins (2).
Interior: AP Images: Bill Chan 17, Amy Sancetta 19;
Newscom: John Dunn/Icon SMI 23, Nick Wosika/Icon
SMI 27; Joe Robbins: 4, 7, 8, 11, 12, 14, 20, 24, 29.

## About the Author

Conor Buckley is a lifelong
baseball fan now studying
for a career in esports. His
books in this series are his first
published works.

## On the Cover

Main photo: Home run hero
Nelson Cruz
Inset: Mariners legend
Ken Griffey, Jr.

# CONTENTS

# GO, MARINERS!

**S**eattle Mariners fans are patient. They have to be. Through 2017, their team had missed the playoffs every year since 2001. That was the longest streak in baseball. Then in 2018, their young stars came through! The Mariners had one of their best seasons in years! What's next for this great team? Let's meet the "M's"!

 *"King" Felix Hernandez is the best Seattle pitcher of all time.*

# WHO ARE THE MARINERS?

**S**eattle plays in the American League (AL). That group is part of Major League Baseball (MLB). MLB also includes the National League (NL). There are 30 teams in MLB. The winner of the AL plays the winner of the NL in the **World Series**.

*Seattle's Kyle Seager makes a great play at third base.* ➤

# WHERE THEY CAME FROM

The Mariners started in 1977. MLB added two new teams that year. The other was the Toronto Blue Jays. The city of Seattle is on the water. Lots of people work and live near the bay and the ocean. The team chose a name to honor that tradition. *Mariner* means a person who works on the sea. The team's **logo** includes a **compass** used by sailors.

◀ *Ken Griffey Jr. is probably the best all-around Mariners player ever.*

# WHO THEY PLAY

The Mariners play 162 games in a season. Seattle plays 81 games at home and 81 games on the road. That's a lot of baseball! They play most of their games against other AL teams. The Mariners are part of the AL West Division. The other AL West teams are the Houston Astros, the Los Angeles Angels, the Oakland Athletics, and the Texas Rangers. Seattle also plays NL teams.

*Mitch Haniger became a star hitter during the 2018 season.* ➤

# WHERE THEY PLAY

**S**eattle is a beautiful city. However, it is also very rainy. How can the Mariners avoid having **rainouts**? Safeco Field has a roof that opens and closes! The stadium opened in 1999. An insurance company called Safeco paid the team to name the stadium. When fans walk in the main gate, they pass under a huge sculpture made of more than 1,000 baseball bats!

◄ *On a sunny day, the roof stays open at Safeco Field.*

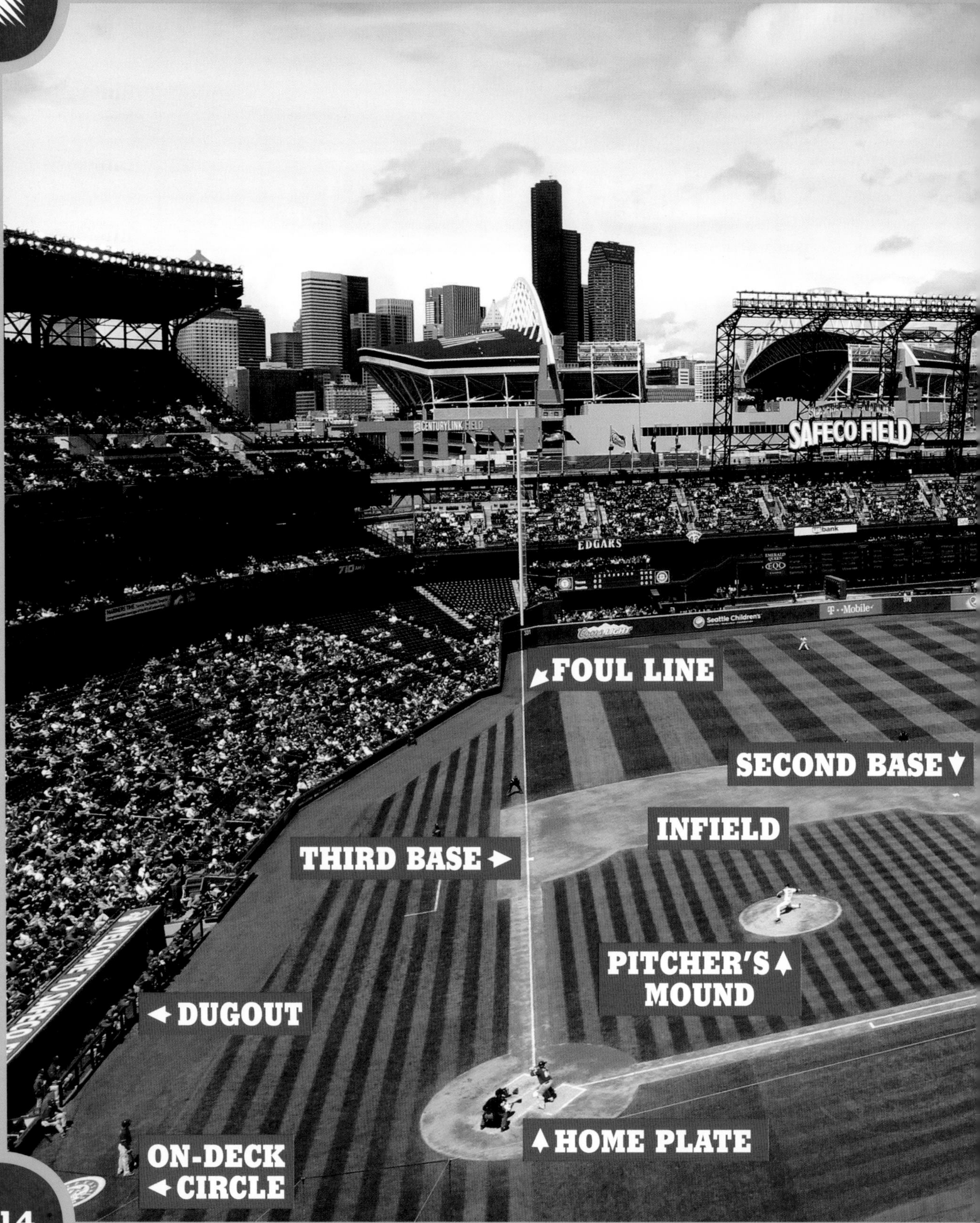

FOUL LINE

SECOND BASE ▼

INFIELD

THIRD BASE ➤

PITCHER'S ▲
MOUND

◄ DUGOUT

▲ HOME PLATE

ON-DECK
◄ CIRCLE

# THE BASEBALL FIELD

**OUTFIELD**

**FOUL LINE**

**FIRST BASE**

**COACH'S BOX**

# BIG DAYS

The Mariners are one of the newest teams in the AL. Still, they have had some memorable moments!

**1995**—The M's made the playoffs for the first time in their history. In five games, they beat the Yankees in the AL Division Series. In Game 5, Edgar Martinez knocked in two runs in the bottom of the 11th inning. Ken Griffey Jr. scored the winning run. His teammates jumped for joy! The Seattle fans went wild! It was the biggest win in team history.

*Safe! Ken Griffey Jr. slides home with the winning run in the biggest game in Mariners history.* ➤

**2011**—The Mariners set an AL record by winning 116 games. (Turn to page 19 for more about 2011!)

**2018**—James Paxton threw a **no-hitter**! The M's beat the Toronto Blue Jays 5–0. The game was in Toronto. Paxton is from Canada. He was the first Canadian to throw a no-hitter in his home nation!

# TOUGH DAYS

**H**ere's a look back at some games and seasons Mariners fans might want to forget!

**1978**—It's tough being a new team. In its second season, Seattle set a team record with 104 losses!

**1986**—Talk about a tough day for hitters. Seattle batters struck out 20 times against Boston's Roger Clemens. The pitcher set an MLB record for strikeouts in a game!

*Ouch! The Mariners were the top team in 2001 . . .*
*until they lost to the Yankees in the playoffs.*

2001—Though Seattle set a league record for wins, it lost in the playoffs. The Yankees beat the M's in five games. It was a tough end to a great season.

# MEET THE FANS!

**S**eattle fans love their M's! They also love the outdoors. The Pacific Northwest is full of great forests. That's why the team's **mascot** is a forest animal. The Mariner Moose keeps things lively at Safeco Field!

◄ *The Mariner Moose looks like it's ready to take the field!*

# HEROES THEN

**K**en Griffey Jr. began his **Hall of Fame** career with the Mariners. Known as "The Kid," he smashed hundreds of homers. His love of the game showed every time he played. Edgar Martinez was one of the best **designated hitters** of all time. Ichiro Suzuki began his career in Japan. He switched to MLB in 2001 and led the AL in hits seven times. He was also a fantastic outfielder. Randy "The Big Unit" Johnson stood six feet, 10 inches! He used his size to be a great fastball pitcher.

*Edgar Martinez was one of the top hitters of the 1990s.* ➤

# HEROES NOW

The most famous player on Seattle today is pitcher Felix Hernandez. Called "King Felix," he holds most of the Mariners pitching records. Home run hero Nelson Cruz has three seasons of 39 or more homers with Seattle. Third baseman Kyle Seager is from a baseball family. His brother Corey is the Los Angeles Dodgers shortstop! Dee Gordon is one of baseball's fastest players. James Paxton is a great pitcher. Edwin Diaz set a team record with 57 saves in 2018.

◄ *Nelson Cruz is a key home run hitter for the Mariners.*

# GEARING UP

Baseball players wear team uniforms. On defense, they wear leather gloves to catch the ball. As batters, they wear hard helmets. This protects them from pitches. Batters hit the ball with long wood bats. Each player chooses his own size of bat. Catchers have the toughest job. They wear a lot of protection.

## THE BASEBALL

The outside of the Major League baseball is made from cow leather. Two leather pieces shaped like 8s are stitched together. There are 108 stitches of red thread. These stitches help players grip the ball. Inside, the ball has a small center of cork and rubber. Hundreds of feet of yarn are tightly wound around this center.

**◀ CATCHER'S MASK AND HELMET**

**▲ CATCHER'S MITT**

**CHEST ▶ PROTECTOR**

**SHIN GUARDS ▶**

# CATCHER'S GEAR

# TEAM STATS

**H**ere are some of the all-time career records for the Seattle Mariners. All of these stats are through the 2018 regular season.

| STOLEN BASES | |
| --- | --- |
| Ichiro Suzuki | 438 |
| Julio Cruz | 290 |

| RBI | |
| --- | --- |
| Edgar Martinez | 1,261 |
| Ken Griffey Jr. | 1,216 |

| STRIKEOUTS | |
| --- | --- |
| Felix Hernandez | 2,467 |
| Randy Johnson | 2,162 |

| HOME RUNS | |
| --- | --- |
| Ken Griffey Jr. | 417 |
| Edgar Martinez | 309 |

| WINS | |
| --- | --- |
| Felix Hernandez | 168 |
| Jamie Moyer | 145 |

| SAVES | |
| --- | --- |
| Kazuhiro Sasaki | 129 |
| Edwin Diaz | 109 |

*Ichiro Suzuki showed off lots of baseball skills for the M's.* ➤

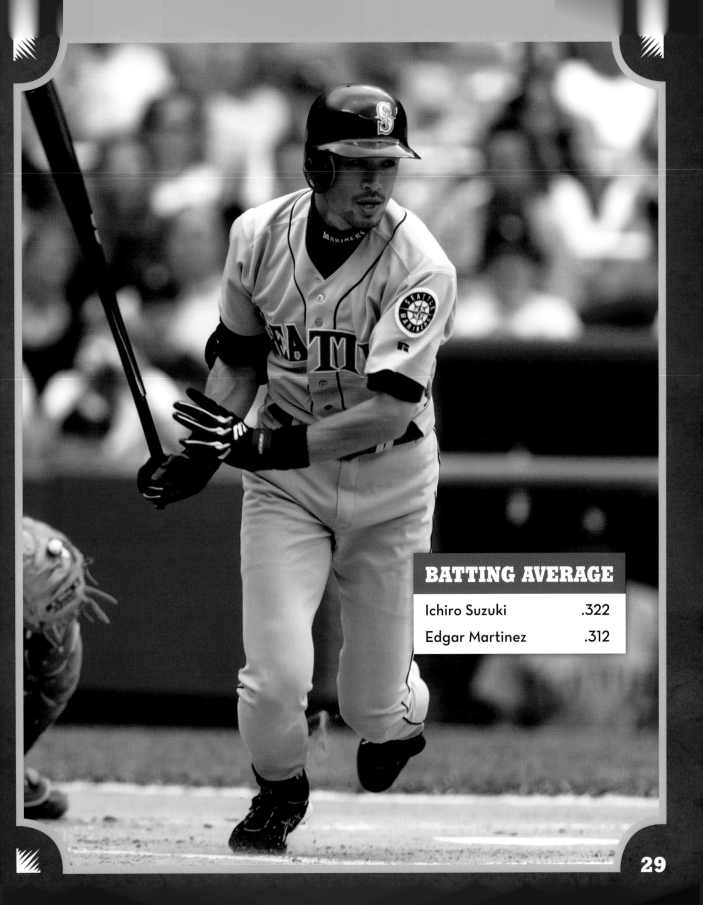

## BATTING AVERAGE

| | |
|---|---|
| Ichiro Suzuki | .322 |
| Edgar Martinez | .312 |

# GLOSSARY

**compass** (KUM-pus) a device that shows direction on Earth

**designated hitter** (DEZ-ig-nate-ed HIT-ter) a player who bats instead of the pitcher in the American League

**Hall of Fame** (HALL UV FAYM) a building in Cooperstown, New York, that honors baseball's greatest players

**logo** (LO-go) a design or illustration that represents a sports team

**mascot** (MASS-cots) a costumed character that helps fans cheer

**no-hitter** (no-HIT-er) a game in which the starting pitcher wins and does not allow a single hit

**rainouts** (RAYN-owtz) games that are cancelled because of rain

**World Series** (WURLD SEE-reez) the annual championship of Major League Baseball

# FIND OUT MORE

## IN THE LIBRARY

Connery-Boyd, Peg. *Seattle Mariners:
The Big Book of Baseball Activities*. Chicago:
Sourcebooks Jabberwocky, 2016.

Leventhal, Josh. *Felix Hernandez (Beisbol!
Latino Heroes of Major League Baseball)*.
Mankato, MN: Black Rabbit Books, 2017.

Savage, Jeff. *Ichiro Suzuki (Amazing Athletes)*.
Minneapolis, MN: Lerner Books, 2014.

## ON THE WEB

Visit our website for links about the Seattle Mariners:
**childsworld.com/links**

*Note to Parents, Teachers, and Librarians: We routinely verify our Web links to make
sure they are safe and active sites. So encourage your readers to check them out!*

# INDEX